엘리트 시선 65

사계절과 기후
Four seasons and climate

장 현 경 시집
Jang Hyunkyung's poetry

엘리트출판사 Elite Publisher

사계절 이야기

사계절과 기후

장현경 시집

- 서문(序文)

사계절 이야기

　우아하고 품격 있는 목련화. 이 땅에 뿌리 내리려 비바람에 온갖 고초를 겪은 산수유꽃. 경사진 곳에서도 고난의 눈물을 견디고 짱짱하게 피어난 진달래꽃. 세월이 흘러 아무 데서나 고혹적이고 예쁘게 잘 자라나, 사랑스러운 눈빛으로 봄 너를 바라보니, 인간 세상 아닌 별천지에 온 듯하네! 봄에 피는 꽃은 아름답기도 하지만 세상을 밝게 해주는 의미도 있다. 탄생 부활의 상징성이 강한 이 봄에 시집 『사계절과 기후』를 상재하게 되어 기쁜 마음 금할 수가 없다.

　이른 아침 장맛비가 어디 가지 말라며 하염없이 창문을 두드린다. 바람은 세고 풀꽃들은 가냘프게 노래하고 뭇 생명을 춤추게 하는 장대비, 집필실로 나를 초대한다. 그리움은 빗물 되어 아, 장맛비! 허기진 배 채워 준 어머니처럼 가슴에 집필 시간으로 쏟아져 자기 내면에서 울리는 무한의 사랑을 노래하고 있다.

　모진 세파에 휩쓸리는 인생의 뒤안길. 자욱한 안개를 담담하게 바라보는 그리움. 핏빛 노을로 덮인 천고마비의 산야, 시린 외로움

에 사무치는 기다림. 격정의 여름이 가고 단풍빛 가득 찬 가을이 내 인생에 자리매김하며, 긴 동면의 시간을 외치고 나니. 알곡의 풍요도 산하의 풍광도 가을은 내일을 예비하기 위한 서곡. 차가운 서리 일찍 내리고 구름 빛 언덕을 지나니, 가을 단풍 완연히 풍긴다.

 단풍 따라왔던 가을 삭풍에 사라지고, 앙상한 나뭇가지 위엔 차가운 별 반짝반짝. 문설주를 넘어선 찬 바람에 창을 여니, 소복이 쌓이는 시린 쌀가루. 별들이 눈발로 흩날리는 밤 골목이 하얗게 덮이면, 화롯불에 구워 먹던 군고구마. 가지마다 쌓인 은색 꽃송이 순백의 사랑으로 무지개 꿈 품고, 세상 후미진 구석을 춤으로 채색해간다.

 늘 따뜻한 성원을 보내주신 가족과 이웃의 지지에 고마운 마음 전하며 청계문학 가족 여러분의 건승을 빕니다. 나의 시편들을 만나는 존경하는 독자님께 건강과 행운이 늘 함께하시기를 기원합니다.

2025년 3월 청계(淸溪) 서재(書齋)에서
자정(紫井) 장현경(張鉉景) 근정(謹呈)

- Preface

Tale of the Four Seasons

Magnolias, elegant and dignified. Cornelian cherry blossoms that have endured all kinds of hardships from wind and rain to take root in this land. Azaleas that have endured tears of hardship and bloomed vigorously even on steep slopes. As time passes, they grow beautifully and captivatingly anywhere, and when I look at you, spring, with loving eyes, it feels like I have come to a different world than the human world! Flowers that bloom in spring are beautiful, but they also have the meaning of brightening the world. I cannot help but be happy to be publishing my poetry collection, Four Seasons and Climate, in this spring, which is strongly symbolic of birth and resurrection.

Early morning rain knocks on the window, telling me not to go anywhere. The wind is strong, the flowers are singing softly, and the heavy rain that makes all living things dance invites me to my study. My longing becomes rainwater, ah, rain! Like a mother who fills my hungry stomach, it pours into my heart as writing time, singing the infinite love that resonates within me.

The back alleys of life, swept by the harsh waves of the world. A longing to calmly look at the thick fog. The mountains and fields covered in bloody sunsets, waiting to be pierced by the cold loneliness. The passionate summer has passed, and autumn, full of maple leaves, has settled into my life, calling out the long hibernation period. The abundance of grains and the scenery of the mountains and rivers, autumn is a prelude to preparing for tomorrow. The cold frost falls early, and as I pass the cloudy hills, autumn leaves are in full bloom.

The autumn wind that followed the maple leaves disappears, and cold stars twinkle on the bare tree branches. When I open the window to the cold wind that goes beyond the doorpost, the cold rice flour that piles up. When the alley is covered in white at night when the stars are scattered like snowflakes, the roasted sweet potatoes that were roasted over the brazier. Silver flower buds piled on each branch, with pure white love, they dream of a rainbow, and color the back corners of the world with dance.

I would like to express my gratitude to my family and neighbors for their constant support and encouragement, and I wish good health to all members of the Cheonggye Literature family. I hope that my respected readers who come across my poems will always be healthy and lucky.

In March 2025, at Cheonggye Library

Jajeong, Jang Hyunkyung Raising

- 서시(序詩)

장맛비

제주도에
오고 있는 비가
북상하여

남해안 지역으로 확대되고
밤사이
북쪽으로 올라가고 있다

내일 새벽에는 충청도로
오후에는
중부지방 대부분 지역에
장맛비가 내릴 예정이다

시간당 30mm의 비가
예정되며
이번 비는
내일 밤에 그칠 예정이다.

– Opening poem

A Rainy Season

In Jeju Island
The rain is coming
Go north

Expanding to the southern coastal area
Overnight
Going up north

Tomorrow morning, to Chungcheong-do
In the afternoon
In most parts of the central region
It's going to be a rainy season

30mm of rain per hour
It is scheduled
This rain
It's expected to end tomorrow night.

contents

□ 서문(序文): 사계절 이야기
(Tale of the Four Seasons) ··· *004*

□ 서시(序詩): 장맛비(A Rainy Season) ··· *010*

제 1부 청명(淸明)

소한(小寒)(Lesser Cold) ··· *018*

대한(大寒)(Great Cold) ··· *022*

입춘(立春)(Onset of Spring) ··· *024*

우수(雨水)(Rainwater) ··· *026*

경칩(驚蟄)(Hard Chip) ··· *028*

춘분(春分)(Vernal Equinox) ··· *030*

청명(淸明)(Qingming) ··· *032*

곡우(穀雨)(Gokwoo) ··· *034*

입하(立夏)(Beginning of summer) ··· *036*

소만(小滿)(Small full) ··· *038*

망종(芒種)(Mangjong) ··· *040*

하지(夏至)(Summer Solstice) ··· *042*

제2부 처서(處暑)

소서(小暑)(Little Heat) ··· *046*

대서(大暑)(The Great Heat) ··· *050*

입추(立秋)(Beginning of Autumn) ··· *054*

처서(處暑)(The Beginning of Summer) ··· *056*

백로(白露)(White Dew) ··· *060*

추분(秋分)(Autumn Equinox) ··· *062*

한로(寒露)(Cold Dew) ··· *064*

contents

상강(霜降)(Frost descending) ··· *066*

입동(立冬)(Beginning of Winter) ··· *070*

소설(小雪)(Little Snowfall) ··· *072*

대설(大雪)(Heavy Snowfall) ··· *074*

동지(冬至)(Winter Solstice) ··· *076*

제 3 부 태풍

양력(陽曆)(Solar Calendar) ··· *080*

음력(陰曆)(Lunar Calendar) ··· *082*

봄(Spring) ··· *084*

여름(Summer) ··· *086*

가을(Fall) ··· *088*

사계절과 기후

겨울(Winter) ··· *090*

태풍(Typhoon) ··· *092*

가뭄(Drought) ··· *094*

제4부 함박눈

초복(初伏)(First Boknal) ··· *098*

중복(中伏)(Second Boknal) ··· *100*

말복(末伏)(Third Boknal) ··· *102*

함박눈(Large Snowflakes) ··· *104*

가루눈(Powder Snow) ··· *106*

진눈깨비(Sleet) ··· *108*

싸락눈(Deep Snow) ··· *110*

contents

제5부 사랑비

사랑비(Love Rain) ⋯ 114

소나기(Shower) ⋯ 116

여우비(Fox Rain) ⋯ 118

장대비(Heavy Rain) ⋯ 120

억수비(A lot of Rain) ⋯ 122

는개비(Neungae Rain) ⋯ 124

이슬비(Drizzling) ⋯ 126

안개비(A Foggy Rain) ⋯ 128

꽃비(Flower Rain) ⋯ 130

뇌우(雷雨)(Thunderstorm) ⋯ 132

먼지잼(Dust Jam) ⋯ 134

제 1 부

청명(淸明)

정갈한 마음으로
하늘을 준비하는 계절
죽은 부지깽이를 꽂아도
싹이 튼다

소한(小寒)

이십사절기 중
스물세 번째 절기
2025. 1. 5.

추위의 절정
소한 때가 가장 춥다

대한이 소한 집에
놀러 갔다가
얼어 죽는다

1월 15일경
한반도에서 가장 추운 날

젊은 추위가 늙은 추위
뺨을 친다

소한 추위는
꾸어다가도 한다

매서운 추위를 이겨
어떤 역경도 이겨낸다.

Lesser Cold

Among the twenty-four solar terms
The Twenty-Third Season
2025. 1. 5.

The peak of cold
Lesser cold is the coldest

In a lesser cold in great cold
I went out to play
I'm freezing to death

Around January 15
The coldest day on the Korean Peninsula

The old cold of the young
Slap the cheek

A lesser cold
I'll do it even if I try

Beat the bitter cold
Overcome any adversity.

대한(大寒)

이십사절기 중
스물네 번째 절기
2025. 1. 20.

큰 추위

소한의 얼음
대한에 녹는다

대한을 마지막으로
겨울이 끝난다

대한 끝에
희망의 봄이 온다.

Great Cold

Among the twenty-four solar terms
The twenty-fourth solar term
2025. 1. 20.

A great cold

Ice of little cold
Melt to the great cold

With the last of great cold
Winter is over

At the end of great cold
Spring of hope is coming.

입춘(立春)

이십사절기의
첫 번째 절기로
새해 시작이며
봄의 시작
2025. 2. 3.

입춘 추위에
김칫독
얼어 터진다

입춘대길(立春大吉)
봄이 시작되니
크게 길하고

건양다경(建陽多慶)
경사스러운 일이
많기를 기원한다.

춘래불사춘(春來不似春)
봄이 왔는데
봄 같지 않다.

Onset of Spring

The twenty-four solar terms
In the first season
It's the start of a new year
The beginning of spring
2025. 2. 3.

In the cold of onset of spring
Kimchi jar
Freeze and burst

Happy New Year
Spring has begun
It's big and long

Konyang Da-kyung
It's a wonderful thing
I hope there are many

Spring has come, but it doesn't seem like spring
Spring has come
It doesn't feel like spring.

우수(雨水)

이십사절기 중
두 번째 절기로
2025. 2. 18.

한 해를 시작하는
봄의 길목

눈과 얼음이 녹아서
비나 물이 되고
날씨가 풀린다

우수 경칩에
대동강 얼음이 녹고
꽃샘추위도 잠시
한파가 사라져

냉이와 쑥부쟁이에
새순이 솟아오르고
나뭇가지에
싹이 돋는다.

Rainwater

Among the twenty-four solar terms
In the second season
2025. 2. 18.

Starting the year
The path of spring

The snow and ice are melting
Become rain or water
The weather is clearing up.

On the excellent day of Keongchip
The ice on the Daedong River is melting
The cold spell is only temporary
The cold wave has disappeared

Cold and mugwort
New shoots are sprouting
On a tree branch
A sprout is sprouting.

경칩(驚蟄)

이십사절기 중
세 번째 절기
2025. 3. 5.

개구리가 깜짝 놀라
활동을 시작하고

고로쇠 수액을
채취하고

달래 냉이가
입맛을 돋운다

만물이 깨어나는 경칩
식물의 싹을 보호하고

흙일을 하면
탈이 없어라.

Hard Chip

During the twenty-fourth season
The third season
2025. 3. 5.

The frog was startled
Start the activity

Gorosh sap
Harvest and

Dallae Naengi
Whets the appetite

The day when all things awaken
Protect the buds of plants

If you do dirt work
Don't have any trouble.

춘분(春分)

이십사절기 중
네 번째 절기로
봄꽃이 만발한다
2025. 3. 20.

봄을 나눈다는 뜻으로
낮과 밤의 길이가
같아지고
농사가 시작되는 달

해가 뜰 때
푸른 구름이 있으면
보리 풍년이 들고

서풍이 불면
보리가 귀하고
북풍이 불면
쌀이 귀하다.

Vernal Equinox

Among the twenty-four solar terms
In the fourth season
Spring flowers are in full bloom
2025. 3. 20.

It means sharing spring
Lead and the length of the night
Becoming the same
The month when farming begins

When the sun rises
If there are blue clouds
The barley harvest is bountiful

When the west wind blows
Barley is precious
When the north wind blows
Rice is expensive.

청명(淸明)

이십사절기 중
다섯 번째 절기
2025. 4. 4.

하늘이 맑아지고
만물의 생기가
왕성해지며

종달새가 울고
오동나무에 꽃이 피고
무지개가 보이는 하늘

정갈한 마음으로
하늘을 준비하는 계절

죽은 부지깽이를 꽂아도
싹이 튼다

개나리 진달래가
꽃망울을 터트리는 들판엔
나비가 날아다니네!

Qingming

Among the twenty-four solar terms
The fifth season
2025. 4. 4.

The sky cleared up
The vitality of all things
In full swing

The swallow is crying
The paulownia tree is in bloom
A sky with a rainbow

With a pure heart
The season of preparing the sky

Even if you stick a dead poker in
Sprouts sprout

Forsythia and azalea
In the fields where flower buds are bursting
A butterfly is flying!

곡우(穀雨)

스물네 절기 중
여섯 번째 절기
2025. 4. 20.

곡식의 싹을
틔우는 봄비가
백곡을 싹트게 하고

땅속 냉기가 사라져
따뜻한 기운이
만들어지는 때

곡우에 가뭄이 들면
땅이 석 자나 마른다

곡우에 비가 오면
풍년이 든다.

Gokwoo

Among the twenty-four solar terms
The sixth season
2025. 4. 20.

The sprouts of grain
The spring rain is falling
Make a hundred grains sprout

The coldness of the ground disappears
Warm air
When it is made

If there is a drought during the Grain Rain
The ground is three feet dry.

If it rains on Grain Rain
The harvest is bountiful.

입하(立夏)

스물네 절기 중
일곱 번째 절기
2025. 5. 5.

여름이 시작되고

보리가 익을 무렵
모를 심고

입하 지나 여름
날씨는 더운데

나무 그늘에서
부채를 부치며
피서를 즐기네

음료수 대신 물 한 잔
책 읽다가 들리는
시원한 바람 소리.

Beginning of summer

Among the twenty-four solar terms
The seventh season
2025. 5. 5.

Summer is starting

When the barley ripens
Planting the unknown

Summer after Beginning of summer
The weather is hot

In the shade of the trees
Waving the fan
Enjoying a vacation

A glass of water instead of a soft drink
I hear this while reading a book
The sound of a cool breeze.

소만(小滿)

스물네 절기 중
여덟 번째 절기
2025. 5. 21.

작은 생명이 가득 차는
오월의 소만

씀바귀가 솟아오르고
아카시아가 만발하며
밀과 보리가 익는다

창문 밖
아름다운 세상에

풍년을 기원하는
모내기

보릿고개 잊어버리고
기쁨의 노래 부르리!

Small full

Among the twenty-four solar terms
The eighth season
2025. 5. 21.

Full of little lives
May's Small full

The snails are rising
Acacias are in full bloom
Wheat and barley ripen

Outside the window
In a beautiful world

Wishing for a good harvest
Transplanting rice seedlings

Forgetting the barley hill
Let us sing a song of joy!

망종(芒種)

스물네 절기 중
아홉 번째 절기
2025. 6. 5.

까끄라기가 있는
곡식의 씨앗

볍씨를 뿌리기에
적당한 시기

보리와 밀을 베고
모내기가 한창일 때

날씨가 더워지고
농작물이 왕성하게
자라는 시기.

Mangjong

Among the twenty-four solar terms
The ninth season
2025. 6. 5.

There is a thorn
Seeds of grain

To sow rice seeds
The right time

Cut barley and wheat
When rice planting is in full swing

The weather is getting warmer
The crops are prosperously
Growing up period.

하지(夏至)

스물네 절기 중
열여섯 번째 절기
2025. 6. 21.

여름의 절정
매미 소리와 더불어
햇감자가 나오고

가뭄에는
기우제를 올리기도 한다

그곳에서
태양에 굶주린 식물들
삼복에 절정을 이룬다

풍년을 그리며
잠들 수 없는 무더위

하지에 비가 내리면
풍년이 든다네!

Summer Solstice

Among the twenty-four solar terms
The sixteenth season
2025. 6. 21.

The height of summer
With the sound of cicadas
The sun-dried potatoes are coming out

In a drought
They also hold a prayer service

In there
Sun-starved plants
It reaches its peak in the three hottest days of summer.

Drawing a good harvest
The heat that keeps me from sleeping

When it rains in Summer solstice
The harvest is bountiful!

사계절과 기후

제2부

처서(處暑)

폭염과 열대야가 사라지며
매미 소리도 감춘다
귀뚜라미 소리가 들려
가을이 왔음을 알리네!

소서(小暑)

스물네 절기 중
열한 번째 날
2025. 7. 7.

작은 더위
장마전선에 걸쳐 있어
습도가 높고
비가 많이 온다

더운 바람이 불어오고
귀뚜라미가 벽을 타고
이곳저곳 다닌다

태풍의 영향으로
폭풍이 일고
폭우로 인해
무더위가 시작된다

보리밭에는
이모작을 짓는다
수박 오이 참외

여름 절기가 시작되는 날
장마철을 알린다.

Little Heat

Among the twenty-four solar terms
The eleventh day
2025. 7. 7.

A little heat
It's across the monsoon front
The humidity is high
It rains a lot

A hot wind is blowing
A cricket climbs the wall
Go here and there

Due to the influence of the typhoon
A storm is brewing
Due to heavy rain
The heat is starting

In the barley field
Make a double cropping
Watermelon cucumber melon

The day when the summer season begins
It signals the rainy season.

대서(大暑)

스물네 절기 중
열두 번째 날
2025. 7. 22.

큰 더위
흙이 습하고
몹시 무더우며
큰 비가 때때로 내린다

참외와 수박이 넘치고
녹음이 우거져
농산물이 풍성하다

삼복더위에
불볕 찜통더위를 겪으며
소나기를 기다린다

하지만
비가 많이 오면
과일의 당도가 떨어지며

가물면
과일 맛이 난다.

The Great Heat

Among the twenty-four solar terms
The twelfth day
2025. 7. 22.

Great heat
The soil is wet
It's very hot
Heavy rain falls occasionally

Melons and watermelons are abundant
The recording is lush
Agricultural products are abundant

In the hot summer heat
Experiencing the scorching heat
Wait for the rain

But
If it rains a lot
The sugar content of the fruit decreases

If it's dry
It tastes like fruit.

입추(立秋)

스물네 절기 중
열세 번째 절기
2025. 8. 7.

가을을 알리는 입추
폭염
열대야
찜통더위

천둥번개가 치면
벼 수확량이 줄고
무더위가 기승을 부린다

칠월 칠석에
서늘한 바람이 불면
가을이 온다

서리 내릴 때
가 보고 싶다
무 배추 감.

Beginning of Autumn

Among the twenty-four solar terms
The thirteenth season
2025. 8. 7.

The beginning of autumn
Heat wave
Tropical night
Sweltering heat

When there is thunder and lightning
Rice yields are decreasing
The heat is on the rise

On the seventh day of the seventh month
When a cool wind blows
Autumn is coming

When the frost falls
I want to go
Radish cabbage persimmon.

처서(處暑)

스물네 절기 중
열네 번째 절기
2025. 8. 23.

아직도
남부는 불타오르는 중
조금 힘들어도
힘을 내 보자

중부는 지낼 만하네
지난밤 선풍기 끄고
이불 덮었다

처서에 비가 오면
흉작을 면하지 못하리

처서가 지나면
파리와 모기가 있는 듯 없는 듯
폭염과 열대야가 사라지며
매미 소리도 감춘다

귀뚜라미 소리가 들려
가을이 왔음을 알리네!

The Beginning of Summer

Among the twenty-four solar terms
The Fourteenth Season
2025. 8. 23.

Still
The South is on fire
Even if it's a little difficult
Let's cheer up

The central part is livable
I turned off the fan last night
Covered with a blanket

If it rains in the beginning of summer
We will not be able to avoid crop failure

After the first rain
There are flies and mosquitoes but they are not there
Heat waves and tropical nights are disappearing
It even hides the sound of cicadas

I hear the sound of crickets
It announces the arrival of autumn!

백로(白露)

스물네 절기 중
열다섯 번째 절기
2025. 9. 7.

농작물에
반짝이는 이슬

장마가 걷히고
쾌청한 날씨가 이어져

기러기 날아오고
제비가 강남으로 돌아가며
뭇 새들이 먹이를 모은다

백로에 비가 내리면
십 리에 천 석이 늘어난다

밤에는 기온이 떨어지고
풀잎엔 이슬이 맺혀
가을 기운이 완연해진다.

White Dew

Among the twenty-four solar terms
The fifteenth season
2025. 9. 7.

In crops
Sparkling dew

The rainy season is over
The clear weather continues

The geese are flying
The swallows return to Gangnam
All the birds gather food.

When it rains on the white heron
A thousand bag increases by ten miles

The temperature drops at night
There is dew on the grass
The autumn spirit is in full swing.

추분(秋分)

스물네 절기 중
열여섯 번째 절기
2025. 9. 23.

여름이 가고
가을이 왔다

우렛소리가 그치고
벌레가 숨는다

낮과 밤의 길이가
같으며
땅 위에 물이 마른다

가을걷이로
마음이 풍성하고

온갖 곡식 열매 맺으니
기쁨이 넘치네!

Autumn Equinox

Among the twenty-four solar terms
The sixteenth season
2025. 9. 23.

Summer is gone
Autumn has come

The thunder stopped
The bug is hiding

The length of day and night
Same as
The water dries up on the ground

For the fall harvest
Rich in heart

It will bear all kinds of grain and fruit.
It's full of joy!

한로(寒露)

스물네 절기 중
열일곱 번째 절기
2025. 10. 8.

밤하늘에 별이
반짝반짝 빛나고

바람이 선선해지며
가을이 깊어지니
찬 이슬이 맺힌다

국화전을 지지고
국화술을 담그며

추어탕이 주는 단백질로
양기를 돕는다

가을 단풍은 짙어만 가고
오곡백과 무르익어
황금빛 들판을 만드네!

Cold Dew

Among the twenty-four solar terms
The seventeenth season
2025. 10. 8.

The stars in the night sky
Shine brightly

The wind is getting cooler
As autumn deepens
A cold dew forms

Supporting the chrysanthemum festival
Soaking chrysanthemums

The protein provided by Chueotang
Helps yang energy

The autumn leaves are getting darker
All the grains are ripe
Creating golden fields!

상강(霜降)

스물네 절기 중
열여덟 번째 절기
2025. 10. 23.

상강에 알밤을
가시 옷으로 감싸고
무더운 여름 거쳐
가을바람 부니
성근 가시 곧 세운다

가을 단풍 색색이 물들 때
가시 옷을 훌훌 벗고
힘차게
누런 풀숲으로 낙하한다

욕심을 내거나 조급해하면
가시에 찔려 피가 흐른다

한 알 두 알
바구니에 담는 기쁨

사랑스럽다
알밤이.

Frost descending

Among the twenty-four solar terms
The eighteenth season
2025. 10. 23.

It's frosty and Chestnuts
Wrapped in thorns
After a hot summer
The autumn wind blows
Several thorns will be erected soon

When the autumn leaves change color
Take off your thorny clothes
Lively
Fall into the yellow grass

If you are greedy or impatient
I got pricked by a thorn and started bleeding.

One, two
Joy in the basket

Lovely
The chestnut.

입동(立冬)

스물네 절기 중
열아홉 번째 절기
2025. 11. 7.

찬 바람 멈춤 없이
가로수 나무로 불어오고

단풍잎 하나둘
바람에 떨어지고

철새가 밤하늘에
무리 지어 떠돈다

가을은 말없이 자리를 비우고
눈 내리는 겨울을 맞는다.

Beginning of Winter

Among the twenty-four solar terms
The nineteenth season
2025. 11. 7.

The cold wind blows without stopping
Blowing through the trees

One or two maple leaves
Falling in the wind

Migratory birds in the night sky
Wander in groups

Autumn leaves silently
We are entering a snowy winter.

소설(小雪)

스물네 절기 중
스무 번째 절기
2025. 11. 22.

소설 추위는 빚내서라도 한다

시래기 걸어 놓고
무말랭이, 곶감 말리기
겨울나기 준비에 바쁘다

얼음이 얼고
첫눈이 내린다

눈꽃 송이 흩날리는
겨울 정취

저 멀리 산속 숲을
하얗게 뒤덮는 눈꽃 세상

창밖에는 하얀 밤!

Little Snowfall

Among the twenty-four solar terms
The twentieth season
2025. 11. 22.

The little Cold is done even if it means borrowing money

Let's hang the dried radish leaves
Dried dried radish and dried Persimmons
Be busy preparing for winter

The ice is frozen
The first snow falls

Snowflakes are falling
Winter mood

The forest in the mountains far away
A world covered in white snow

Outside the window is a white night!

대설(大雪)

스물네 절기 중
스물한 번째 절기
2025. 12. 7.

눈이 많이 내리면
풍년이 든다

중부지방을 중심으로
전국에
대설 특보가 발효되어

온 국민이
기쁜 마음으로
쌓이는 눈을 치우고 있다

드물게
폭설이 내려

대설 경보가
유지 중이다.

Heavy Snowfall

Among the twenty-four solar terms
The twenty-first season
2025. 12. 7.

If it snows a lot
Have a good harvest

Focusing on the central region
All over the country
A heavy snow warning has been issued

The whole nation
With a happy heart
Clearing away the accumulating snow

Rarely
It's snowing heavily

Heavy snow warning
It is being maintained.

동지(冬至)

스물네 절기 중
스물두 번째 절기
2025. 12. 22.

밤이 가장 길고
낮이 가장 짧은 날

동지는 작은 설
태양이 죽음으로부터
부활하는 날

오랜 세월에 걸쳐
내린 함박눈

한겨울에 팥죽 먹고
소원 이루어져

빛이 반짝반짝.

Winter Solstice

Among the twenty-four solar terms
The 22nd season
2025. 12. 22.

The night is the longest
The shortest day

Winter solstice is a small New Year's Day
The sun from death
The day of the resurrection

Over the years
The snow fell

Eating red bean porridge in the middle of winter
Wish come true

The light is shining.

사계절과 기후

제3부

태풍

우르르 쾅 쾅!
태풍에는 눈이 있어
비바람을 이끌고
길고 짧은 생을 살다가

양력(陽曆)

태양의 움직임을
기준으로 삼은 달력

서구 문명의 영향으로
우리나라는 1896년
을미개혁 때
양력을 도입

지구가 태양을 한 바퀴 도는데
걸리는 시간을
일 년으로 하는 달력

계절과 날씨에 잘 맞고
농사에 도움이 되는 달력.

Solar Calendar

The movement of the sun
Calendar as a reference

Under the influence of Western Civilization
Our country in 1896
During the Eulmi Reform
Introducing the solar calendar

The Earth revolves around the sun
The time it takes
Calendar for one year

It suits the season and weather well
A calendar conductive to farming.

음력(陰曆)

달이 차고
기울어지는 현상을
기초로 하여 만든 달력

달이 지구를 한 바퀴 돌아
걸리는 시간을
기준으로 만든 달력

음력 한 달을 기준으로
초승달에서
상현 그믐까지
모양을 바꾼다

설날은 명절이다
새해 새달의 첫날로.

Lunar Calendar

The moon is full
The phenomenon of tilting
Calendar made based on

The moon goes around the earth
The time it takes
Calendar made based on standard

Based on the lunar month
In the crescent moon
Until the last day of the month
Change the shape

Lunar New Year is a national holiday
On the first day of the new year.

봄

우아하고
품격 있는 목련화

이 땅에 뿌리 내리려
비바람에
온갖 고초를 겪은 산수유꽃

경사진 곳에서도
고난의 눈물을 견디고
짱짱하게 피어난 진달래꽃

세월이 흘러
아무 데서나
고혹적이고 예쁘게
잘 자라나

경건한 마음으로
사랑스러운 눈빛으로
봄
너를 바라본다.

Spring

Elegant
Magnolia of elegance

To put down roots in this land
In the wind and rain
The cornelian flower that have endured all kinds of hardships

Even on a steep slope
Endure the tears of suffering
Azaleas in full bloom

As time goes by
Anywhere
Alluring and pretty
Grow up well

With a devout heart
With loving eyes
Spring
I look at you.

여름

어두컴컴하더니
하염없이 장맛비가
어디 가지 말라며
창문을 두드린다

바람은 세고
풀꽃은 가냘프게 노래하고
뭇 생명을 춤추게 하는 장대비
집필실로 나를 초대한다

그리움은 빗물 되어

아, 장맛비!
허기진 배 채워 준 어머니처럼
가슴에 집필 시간으로 쏟아지네!

Summer

It was dark
It keeps raining
Don't go anywhere
knock on the window

The wind is strong
The flowers of the grass sing softly
Heavy rain that makes all living things dance
Invite me to the writing room

Longing becomes rain

Ah, It's a good rain!
Like a mother who fills a hungry stomach
In the chest
It's pouring down with writing time!

가을

모진 세파에 휩쓸리는
인생의 뒤안길

자욱한 안개를
담담하게 바라보는 그리움

핏빛 노을로 덮인 천고마비의 산야
시린 외로움에 사무치는 기다림

격정의 여름이 가고
단풍빛 가득 찬 가을이
내 인생에 자리매김하며
긴 동면의 시간을 외치고 나니

알곡의 풍요도 산하의 풍광도
가을은
내일을 예비하기 위한 서곡

등 뒤 내 그림자를
돌아보게 하는 선지자!

Fall

Being swept away by the harsh waves
The back alleys of life

Thick fog
Longing to be looked at calmly

The mountains and fields of the heavenly paralysis
covered with blood-red sunset
Waiting filled with bitter loneliness

The passionate summer is gone
Autumn full of maple leaves
Taking hold in my life
After shouting out the long hibernation period

The abundance of grain and the beautiful scenery of the mountains and rivers
Autumn is
Prelude to prepare for tomorrow

My shadow behind my back
The prophet who makes us look back!

겨울

나뭇가지마다
쌓인 은색 꽃송이

이른 아침
모자를 눌러쓰고
운동 삼아
산책하니

허허로운 거리마다
눈에 들어오는 눈꽃

아침을 열며
눈이 시리도록
반기는
아름다운 눈꽃.

Winter

On every branch
Stacked silver flower buds

Early morning
Put your hat on
For exercise
Going for a walk

In every empty street
Snowflake in the eye

Opening the morning
My eyes hurt
Welcoming
Beautiful snow flowers.

태풍

우르르 쾅 쾅!

태풍에는 눈이 있어
비바람을 이끌고
길고 짧은 생을 살다가

갈 길을 찾아
이리저리
멋대로 길을 내며 달린다

힘 있는 태풍도
눈을 잘못 굴리면
머지않아 사라진다

시간이 흐른 뒤
새 생명이 탄생하여
깨끗한 지구, 신선한 공기로
흔적을 남긴다.

Typhoon

Wooroo boom boom!

The typhoon has eyes
Leading the wind and rain
After living a long and short life

Find your way
Back and forth
Run wildly on your own path

Even powerful typhoons
If you roll your eyes wrong
It will disappear soon

After some time has passed
A new life is born
Clean Earth, Fresh Air
It leaves a trace.

가뭄

봄과 여름
가을이

태양과 구름
바람에

비를 내리라고

땀을 뻘뻘

하늘을
우러러본다.

Drought

Spring and summer
Autumn

The sun and clouds
In the wind

Make it rain

Sweating profusely

The sky
Look up.

사계절과 기후

제4부

함박눈

굵고 탐스럽게
흩날리는 하얀 꽃송이
함박꽃을 닮았네

초복(初伏)

흐리고 비 와도
인삼과 영계로
삼계탕 만들어
그대와 나누고 싶다

무더위의 시작
더위를 이기기 위해
산간 계곡을 찾는다

상처 난 산수(傘壽)
아직도 젊었는가?

오늘은 초복
추어탕이 기다리고 있네!

First Boknal

Even if it's cloudy and rainy
With ginseng and chicken
Make Samgyetang
I want to share it with you

The beginning of the heat
To beat the heat
Find a mountain valley

80 year old with scars
Are you still young?

Today is Chobok
Chueotang is waiting!

중복(中伏)

오늘은 중복
한여름 무더위가
절정에 이르는 시기

오늘 밤 열대야가
악몽에 시달리게 하고

등줄기 흐르는 땀
온몸에 퍼져도
겁 안 난다

내 마음에
생각만으로도 기분 좋은
그대가 있으니까

강으로
바닷가로
찜통더위가 설치고 다녀도
가을은 찾아오리!

Second Boknal

Today, It's overlapping
The midsummer heat
The climax of the season

It's a tropical night tonight
It gives me nightmares

Sweat running down my back
Even if it spreads throughout the body
I'm not scared

In my heart
Just thinking about it makes me feel good
Because you are here

To the river
To the beach
Even though the heat is stifling
Autumn will come!

말복(末伏)

말복을 맞아
해는 아직 길고

보양 음식의 대표
점심 특선
삼계탕

저녁 특선
천연 피로해소제
문어

글을 아는 물고기
대왕문어

여름을 건강하게
장어구이.

Third Boknal

Welcome to the last days of summer
The days are still long

Representative of nutritious food
Lunch special
Samgyetang

Dinner special
National fatigue reliever
Octopus

A fish that knows how to write
A giant octopus

Stay healthy in summer
Grilled eel.

함박눈

굵고 탐스럽게
흩날리는 하얀 꽃송이
함박꽃을 닮았네

펑펑
소리 없이
쏟아지는 함박눈

눈발이 거세지고
폭설이 난무하는 언덕에
그리움이 쌓이고 쌓여

온 세상이
새하얗게 변하네!

Large Snowflakes

Thickly and covetously
Fluttering white flowers
It looks like a daisy

Boom boom
Without a sound
Pouring sleet

The snow is falling heavily
On a hill covered with heavy snow
Longing piles up and piles up

The whole world
It's turning pure white!

가루눈

온도가 낮고
수증기가 적을 때

가루처럼
작은 알갱이로
흩날리는 눈

추울 때는
눈송이를 만들지 못해

굳어 있는 눈 위에
팔랑팔랑
가루눈이 내린다

산간벽지에
작은 얼음 알갱이
수북이 쌓일 때
스키 타면 좋겠네!

Powder Snow

The temperature is low
When there is little water vapor

Like powder
In small grains
Fluttering snow

When it's cold
I can't make snowflakes

On the frozen snow
Flapping
It's snowing powdery snow

In a mountainous area
Small ice grains
When the water piles up
I wish I could ski!

진눈깨비

아침에 일어나 보니
진눈깨비가 내리다가
함박눈이 내린다

진눈깨비보다
더 큰 눈송이는 우박

비가 진눈깨비가 되거나
진눈깨비가 비나 눈이 된다

비가 반
눈이 반인 진눈깨비

쌓인 눈도
얼음도 없어
추억이 없다.

Sleet

When I woke up in the morning
It was snowing
It snows in large flakes

Rather than sleet
Larger snowflakes are hail

The rain turns to sleet
The sleet turns into rain or snow

It's half raining
Half-snow sleet

The accumulated snow too
There is no ice
I have no memories.

싸락눈

겨울철에
자연이 만든 싸락눈

사락사락 싸락눈이
땅 위에
쌀알처럼 구르며 쌓인다

장독대에
하얀 꽃을 피운다
정겹다

바람 따라
날아 온 겨울 철새가
싸락눈 내리는 풍경과
어우러져
허전한 마음을 달래주고 있다

강물은 유유히 흐르고.

Deep Snow

In winter
Nature-made snow

Snowflakes falling
On the ground
Roll and pile up like grains of rice

In the Jangdokdae
It blooms white flowers
It's nice

Follow and wind
The winter migratory birds that flew in
A landscape with falling snow
Blend together
Soothing my empty heart

The river flows leisurely.

사계절과 기후

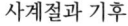

제5부

사랑비

가랑비가 내리던 날
네 곁에서
마음 가득
머무르고 싶어라!

사랑비

비가
부슬부슬
내리던 날

우산도 없이
비를 맞고 싶어
거리를 거닐어 본다

빗소리가 좋아
비에 흠뻑 젖고 싶어
그대를 바라본다

가랑비가 내리던 날
네 곁에서
마음 가득
머무르고 싶어라!

Love Rain

Rain
Drizzle
The day it rained

Without an umbrella
I want to get rained on
Take a stroll down the street

I like the sound of rain
I want to get drenched in rain
I look at you

A day when drizzle was falling
By your side
Full of heart
I want to stay!

소나기

갑자기 세차게 내리다가
비가 그친다

천둥소리에
우산 없이 가다가
검은 구름이 반가운 척
곁에 다가와

후다닥
마른 땅에
먼지를 일으켜

바람과 손잡고
슬그머니 사라진다.

Shower

It suddenly started pouring down heavily
The rain stops

At the sound of thunder
Going without an umbrella
Black clouds pretend to be welcome
Come near me

In a hurry
On dry land
Raise dust

Hand in hand with the wind
It disappears quietly.

여우비

햇살이 쨍쨍
내리쬐는 오후

저 멀리
잿빛 구름이
바람에 밀려
쏜살같이 다가온다

찬 빗방울이
우두둑 떨어질 때

고개 들어
다시 바라보니

저쪽 하늘에
뜬
아름다운 무지개.

Fox Rain

The sun is shining brightly
A blazing afternoon

Over there
The gray clouds
Blown by the wind
Coming at a rapid pace

Cold raindrops
When it falls down with a thud

Lift your head
Looking back again

In the sky over there
Floating
A beautiful rainbow.

장대비

이른 아침
호우주의보가
내려진 중부지방에

굵고 거센 장대비가
쏟아지면서

마음을
시원하게 하는 빗소리
울려 퍼진다

도로 곳곳이
통제되고

저녁 무렵
기상청에서
호우주의보를 해제했다.

Heavy Rain

Early morning
Heavy rain advisory
In the central region where it was established

Heavy, heavy rain
As it pours

My heart
The refreshing sound of rain
It resonates

All over the road
Controlled

In the evening
From the Meteorological Agency
The heavy rain advisory has been lifted.

억수비

물을 퍼붓듯이
세차게 내리는 억수비

강한 바람이
잠시
지속되다가
갑자기 멈추는 현상

번개와 천둥이 치며
우레소리가 들려 온다

골목길이
강물로 변해
스트레스가 쌓인다.

A Lot of Rain

Like pouring water
A torrential downpour

The strong wind
For a moment
Continued
Sudden stop phenomenon

There was lightning and thunder
I hear thunder.

The alleyway
Turn into a river
Stress builds up.

는개비

안개비보다
조금 굵고
이슬비보다
약간 가는 는개비를
그리며

부슬부슬 내리는
네 포근한 자태에
내 마음도 흐뭇하구나

추억처럼 다가오는 는개비
우산 없이 함께 걸어간다

한여름 산야(山野)가
무성하더라도
는개비 흩날릴 때는
온 누리가 신비한 세계.

Neungae Rain

Than foggy rain
A little thick
Than drizzle
A small piece of neungae rain
Missing you

It's drizzling
In your warm figure
My heart is also happy

Neungae rain approaching like a memory
Walking together without an umbrella

The mountains and fields in midsummer
Even if It's lush
When It's flying like neungae rain
The whole world is a mysterious world.

이슬비

이슬비가 내리네
부슬부슬
유리창을 적시네

하얗게 흩날리며
얼굴을 더듬네

이슬비 맞으며
터벅터벅 걷는다

이슬비가
소식 전하려
안개처럼 내린다.

Drizzling

It's drizzling
Drizzle
Wet the window

Fluttering white
Touching my face

In the drizzle
Walk with plodding steps

Drizzle
To tell the news
It falls like fog.

안개비

안개비가 뿌옇게 내리던 날
옷이 젖어 있어도
비가 오는 줄 모르고
걷고 있었다

안개비를 보며
젖은 옷을 벗고
우산을 펼쳤다

문득 돌아보니
눈이 부시게
보석 같은 안개비가 내려

사랑하는 임에게
안개비
가슴에 안겨 드리리

그 임 오시는 길에
안개비 맞으며
영원히
그 삶을 사랑하리.

A Foggy Rain

A day when misty rain was falling
Even if your clothes are wet
Without knowing it was going to rain
I was walking

Watching the misty rain
Take off your wet clothes
I opened my umbrella

Suddenly I looked back
Dazzlingly
Jewel-like misty rain falls

To my beloved
A foggy rain
I'll hold you in my heart

On the way there
In the misty rain
Forever
I will love that life.

꽃비

꽃비가 내린 후
아지랑이 하늘거리는 봄날

바위틈에
진달래 피고
개나리 샛노랗다

감미로운 향기를 품은 매화
빛깔이 고운 이화
멀리 있어도 흩날리는 꽃비
눈에 잘 보이고

화사한 벚꽃과 살구꽃
활짝 피어
바람에 미소 짓네!

언덕으로 달리는 봄
향기를 가득 담은 꽃비에
잠시 머문다.

Flower Rain

After the flower rain
A spring day with azure skies

In the crevice of the rock
Azaleas are blooming
Forsythia is bright yellow

Plum blossoms with a sweet fragrance
Beautifully colored pear blossoms
Even though It's far away, the flower rain is falling
It's visible to the eyes

Brilliant cherry blossoms and apricot blossoms
In full bloom
Smile in the wind!

Spring running up the hill
In the flower rain full of fragrance
Stay for a while.

뇌우(雷雨)

천둥번개가
돌풍과 함께
내리는 빗소리

스트레스 해소하려
걸음을 멈추네

뇌우를 동반한 먹구름이
세찬 비바람에
우수수 떨어지는 꽃바람으로

까마득한 지난날이
시냇물과 졸졸 졸
스쳐 흘러가네!

Thunderstorm

Thunder and lightning
With the gust of wind
The sound of falling rain

To relieve stress
Stop walking

Dark clouds with thunderstorm
In the heavy rain and wind
With the wind blowing corn flowers

The distant past
Stream and trickle trickle
It just passes by!

먼지잼

'먼지를 재운다'
압축하여 쓴 글

오랜 가뭄으로
메마른 땅에
흩날리는 먼지를
가라앉힐 정도로
조금 내리는 비

미세 먼지는
발암 물질로
호흡기 질환에 미치는
영향이 커

분무기로 쉽게
세척이 가능하여
방충망만 깨끗해도
건강에 도움 되네!

Dust Jam

'Raise the dust'
Compressed writing

Due to a long drought
In the dry land
The scattered dust
Enough to sink
A little rain

Fine dust
As a carcinogen
Effects on respiratory diseases
The impact is huge

Easy with a sprayer
Because it is washable
Even if only the mosquito net is clean
It's good for your health!

사계절과 기후

초판인쇄 2025년 3월 12일 초판발행 2025년 3월 18일

지은이 장현경
펴낸이 장현경   펴낸곳 엘리트출판사
편집 디자인 마영임
등록일 2013년 2월 22일 제2013-10호

서울특별시 광진구 긴고랑로15길 11 (중곡동)
전화 010-5338-7925
E-mail : wedgus@daum.net

정가 15,000원

ISBN 979-11-87573-49-4 03810